THINGS I'M AVOIDING DOING

A GUIDE TO OVERCOMING PROCRASTINATION AND GETTING [SH]IT DONE

MICHAEL NEILL

CAFFEINE FOR THE SOUL PRESS

CONTENTS

INTRODUCTION

"The law of nature is: Do the thing and you will have the power, but they who do not do the thing have not the power."

-Ralph Waldo Emerson

———

This little book is about liberation. I put it together to free us up from the tyranny of our own to-do lists - what the psychoanalyst Karen Horney called "the tyranny of the shoulds".

It was born in a hot tub in Austin, TX a few Thanksgivings ago. My 20-something year old son Oliver was complaining about how long his to-do list had become, how much stuff he was avoiding doing, and how badly he was feeling about himself for not doing it.

As I listened, I quickly realized that everything he was saying was true for me too. So instead of offering him some quasi-wise piece of "Dad" advice, I suggested that I would put together a program for the two of us to do that would clear our lists and free our minds by the end of the year.

Since I have a fairly large online community at www.michaelneill.org, I invited anyone who wanted to join us for a four week challenge to come along for the ride. Each day, I posted a different tip, trick, or hack to not only get [sh]it done but to enjoy the process. The goal was to reclaim some of the mental bandwidth that was getting eaten up with blame, shame, worry, and all the other mental gymnastics that take up the very energy that makes getting stuff done surprisingly simple and straightforward.

I've adapted the program slightly for this book, both to incorporate things I've seen in sharing my productivity programs with individual and corporate clients in the intervening years and to make it even easier to put into practice.

Here are a few guidelines before we get started:

1. This book is about getting [sh]it done, not learning *how* to get [sh]it done. If you have a choice between getting something off your list or reading about how to get something off your list, get the damn thing off your list and you can always come back and read about it later.

2. We'll be focused on the things you're avoiding doing more than the things you just haven't got around to yet. How do you know the difference? What you're avoiding doing feels bad when you think about it.

3. This is not "a system" that you need to learn or practice. It is a collection of simple truths about the nature of human beings and how the way we think about things makes it easier (or usually more difficult) to get them done.

Because of this, I recommend you read them in whatever way appeals to you:

- You can read and where relevant apply each day's lesson over the next four weeks, one day at a time.
- You can read through the whole book in one go, then go back and apply any of the ideas that grabbed your attention or intrigued you along the way.

- You can scan the table of contents and choose the topic that seems most relevant to you in the moment you are currently in.

Whatever strategy you choose, it's important to not let finishing the book become more important than clearing your list. We'll talk more about why that's so on day one of the program.

In the meantime, here's all you need to do to get started:

Make a list of everything you can think of that you've been putting off, avoiding doing, or that's simply pre-occupying your brain and making life seem overwhelming.

(Please note this isn't meant to be a comprehensive "to-do" list - you'll probably always have one of those. This is simply a list of your backlog of things you've been avoiding doing that are taking up your time and/or mental bandwidth.)

You can add and subtract things from this list at any time, so think of it more as a working draft than a definitive inventory.

When you've got your list, you can get started on day one. (Though in all honesty, if making the list starts to feel like another item on your list, skip it for now and get stuck in anyways.)

Have fun, learn heaps, and happy exploring!

With all my love,

Michael

WEEK ONE: THE BASICS

"Someday is just a thought."
-Eirik Grunde Olsen

DAY ONE: THE THREE KEYS TO GETTING STUFF DONE

I n over thirty years of coaching people, I've come to see that there are two primary approaches people take to getting things done in life. The first is "fixed means, variable outcome", which I tend to illustrate like this:

Fixed means, variable outcome

In this approach, there is a right and/or best way to do something, and you accept that when you do things the right/best way, it will work great for some people but not so well for others and it will work great in some situations but not so much in others.

The other approach is "fixed outcome, variable means", which I tend to illustrate like this:

Fixed outcome, variable means

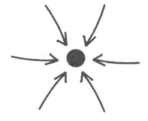

In this approach, we abandon the search for the right or even best way and simply play around with it until something works.

Here's the first key:

Just because something works doesn't make it the right

or even best way to do it - it just means it worked to generate the desired outcome this time around.

———

Here's the second key:

When it comes to getting stuff done - particularly the stuff we've been avoiding doing - the search for the "right way" or "best way" is one of the best ways to avoid doing it!

So as you go through this 30-day challenge, I encourage you to experiment with a "Fixed outcome, variable means" approach. The fixed outcome is whatever you've been putting off that you want to get done; the variable means will be whatever comes up or comes to mind to do.

Here's the final key, and the closest thing to a prescription you'll find in all 30 days of the challenge:

When something works, feel free to do more of it; when it doesn't, feel free to do something else instead.

———

What did you get off your list today?

DAY TWO: HAVE TO, WANT TO, OR SHOULD?

When it comes to getting stuff off of our getting stuff done lists, it's sometimes helpful to delineate between things that *have* to get done, things you *want* to get done, and things you think you *should* get done.

────

1. Have to

When we say we "have to" get something done, what we usually mean is that there is some real-world consequence to not getting it off our list that we would prefer to avoid. Those real-world consequences are either real-world practical (like getting evicted for not paying your rent or mortgage) or mental/emotional (like getting stressed out because you still haven't done something you promised someone you'd do and worrying that they'll be mad at you).

For the purposes of this 30-day challenge, I recommend only including "have to's" that have real-world practical consequences. We'll talk about the mental/emotional ones in the "Should" section below.

———

2. Want to

Nobody else can tell you what you actually want to get done. Real wants come with a simple feeling of desire and no particular story about "why". Simple desire seems to be one of the ways we are designed to navigate life, but because most of us have learned not to trust it as sufficient motivation, we tend to try to turn all of our "want to's" into "have to's"

One way we do this is by adding in a scary story about the consequences of not doing it; the other is by adding in sexy story about the benefits of doing it. While it's not always obvious to us what stories we're telling ourselves about the things on our list, the fact that we continue to put them off is a pretty solid indication that we've got them.

Here's a simple rule of thumb:

The number of reasons you have for doing something is inversely proportional to how much you actually want to do it.

---

3. Should

Generally speaking, when the imagined consequence of not doing something is that we think we're going to feel bad about not doing it, we tell ourselves that it's something we "should" do, even though we don't really have to or want to.

I will admit to a strong personal bias against people "shoulding" all over themselves. Generally speaking, I've seen more people procrastinate on their "shoulds" than over any number of simple desires or genuine needs.

Here's today's mini-experiment:

- Go through your list of things you've been putting off that you want to get done during the course of this book.

- Put an "H" next to the real-world practical conse-quence "have to's", a "W" next to the ones you'd simply like to get done, and an "S" next to the one's that you feel like you should do but you don't really want to and there are no real world practical consequences to not getting them done

- Consider just removing all the "shoulds" from your list without doing anything else about them. If you happen to get them done anyways (or at some point you find yourself actually wanting to get them done), by all means do them

Having said all that (and as I will be reminding you throughout our time together), I'm suggesting using a fixed outcome, variable means approach to getting things done and off your list. So if you find yourself easily moving forward on the things you "should" do, by all means feel free to leave them on your list!

———

What did you get off your list today?

DAY THREE: FEELING VS. DOING

A number of years ago, I began working on the manuscript for my sixth book, *Creating the Impossible: A 90-Day program to get your dreams out of your head and into the world.* I had already been running an online version of the program for close to a decade, so I felt confident that this would be a relatively easy book to write. For the first time in memory, I didn't freak out as the deadline approached, recognizing that my fears were made of scary thoughts and my track record spoke for itself.

And then, for the first time ever, I missed a publication deadline. Hay House very kindly moved the release of the book back by a couple of months to give me more than enough time to finish. And then I missed the second deadline.

I felt oddly liberated, finally understanding the words of Douglas Adams, author of *The Hitchhiker's Guide to the Galaxy* series, who said "I love deadlines. I love the whooshing sound they make as they go by."

It was around that time that my agent phoned me to check in on how it was all going.

"Great", I replied. "I've never felt so chilled and at peace around missing a deadline."

"That's wonderful", he said with quiet humor in his voice. "How's the book coming?"

And that was the moment where I fell down the staircase of insight and bumped my head on a deeper truth.

Our common cultural mythology around getting stuff done is that what we do or don't do is a huge determinant of how we feel, and how we feel in turn determines what we do. We feel pressure, stress, guilt, and shame when we're not doing what we think we should, and we attempt to use those feelings to compel ourselves into action.

But what I saw as clear as day was that what we do and how we feel are two completely independent variables. I'd had plenty of experiences of feeling stressed out and taking action; I now had an experience of not feeling stressed out and not taking action. But that didn't mean that the two things had a cause-effect relationship.

I recognized that there had been any number of times where I felt great and got a ton done, and an equal number of times where I'd felt stressed and pressured and gotten a ton done. And while in this instance my inactivity coincided with a feeling of ease and comfort, I had no shortage of examples of inactivity accompanied by feelings of discomfort.

Suddenly, I realized a screamingly obvious truth:

If I do what there is to do, things get done; if I don't, they usually don't.

At some level, I already knew this. For over thirty years, my go to move as a coach when a client complains about putting off a task as a symptom of procrastination is to ignore their complaint and tell them to call me back when the task is done. Inevitably, things that had previously seemed impossible for them to get themselves to do, like paying bills, having a difficult conversation, or getting started on a big project, find themselves getting done without anything having to change in my client's psychology,

But because I hadn't seen the principles behind it, I thought of it as a cool trick – a way of getting people into action when it worked and annoying the heck out of them when it didn't.

I could now see a deeper truth:

What gets done has everything to do with what we do and almost nothing to do with how we feel.

Whether our job is writing a book, hitting a golf ball, building a house, or building a business, our results will be largely a function of the writing, hitting, and building that we do regardless of how we happen to be feeling while we do it.

I've come to love the fact that when it comes to getting things done in the world, I can do what there is to do regardless of how enlightened I happen to be feeling from day to day.

Here's a question for you regardless of how you feel when you look at your list:

How's the "book" coming?

———

What did you get off your list today?

DAY FOUR: NEXT STEP OR MINI-PROJECT?

"To-Do" lists are funny creatures. On the one hand, they can be incredibly helpful ways of keeping our heads clear and present by giving us a more stable and reliable storage shelf than the three pound cauliflower shaped lump of grey matter inside our skulls. On the other hand, they can become an endless justification for always feeling like no matter how much you get done, there's always more to do.

One simple distinction that most people find helpful if and when they get stuck on something on their list is to notice "is this an actual action or is it a mini-project'?"

An action is something that can just be done (or not done) right now; a mini-project sounds a bit like an action but actually involves multiple steps.

For example, let's take a surprisingly common item on someone's list - to write a book. Even if I was talking to Isaac Asimov (author of over 400 books) or Ryoki Inoue (author of over 1075 published titles), they couldn't "just do it" while I was waiting. There would be ideas to be brainstormed, research to be done, and periods of writing, reflection, and editing to be completed.

Or another common list item for businesses that is often procrastinated on or avoided – "Sort out unpaid invoices". While it's possible that any one of the unpaid invoices on a company's ledger might be sorted out with one phone call, the reality is that there are probably multiple papers to be sorted through, calls to be made, invoices to be sent, and messages to be followed up on before we could cross the item off our list.

To make this distinction practical with your own "Things I'm avoiding doing" list, run through it and see what's an actual action item and what's a mini-project disguised as an action item.

- For each action item, do it or leave it for now.

- For each project, jot down the next step –
  what's the very first action that you could take

right now to move forward on your mini-project? Then either take it or leave it for now.

————

What did you get off your list today?

DAY FIVE: A MAGIC FORMULA FOR GETTING [SH]IT DONE

If there was such a thing as a "magic formula" for getting things done, it would look something like this:

T (time) +A (attention) =R (results)

In other words, if you want to get something done, you'll usually get it done faster and better if you give yourself enough time and attention to do it.

The opposite is equally true – if you're consistently not getting something done, you're almost certainly not giving yourself enough time, giving it enough attention, or both.

A simple way to check this for yourself is to take something on your list and notice if you're trying to get *through* it or if you're giving yourself the time and space to get *into* it instead. While it may sometimes seem to take longer to get into things than to just soldier on through them, when you're consistently putting something off, it's often because you're spending more time thinking about it than doing it.

―――――

What did you get off your list today?

DAY SIX: BILLABLE HOURS

T he very fact that you're reading this book means that you've at least begun prioritizing the things you'd previously been avoiding doing.

Here's a simple exercise you can do to get a better sense of how far up or down the ladder of priorities your list is currently sitting. You can do this exercise for any individual goal or project on your list and/or you can do it for the list as a whole...

1. Just for fun, guesstimate the number of "billable hours" you've put into your goal, project, or list over the past three weeks. This is the number of hours that you would feel comfortable billing a client for if they were paying you to work on it.

2. Starting today (and over the rest of the week if you're

up for it), log all your "billable" time working on your item or list.

In my experience, you'll fairly quickly notice one of two things.

Either you really are putting in the hours and what you're working on is just something that requires more time than you thought or hoped, OR you'll realize that until you make this a bit more or a priority (by spending a bit more time and attention on it), there's no point in beating yourself up about not getting it done.

———

What did you get off your list today?

DAY SEVEN: DO YOU REALLY NOT HAVE THE TIME?

I don't come off very well in this story, but not long after my family and I moved to America, I sat down to prepare a log of how much time I was spending on all my work projects so that I could persuade my wife I really didn't have "extra time" to help out with the house and kids. To my dismay, I found I was spending less than two hours a day actually working and ten to twelve hours thinking about what there was to be done.

While I was aware that giving myself time for reflection opened me up to creativity, I was equally aware that obsessively thinking about the same things for days on end was a great way of closing down the creative flow. I never did show my wife my time log, but I started volunteering to help out with a lot more tasks around the house. And as soon as I had less time or inclination to overthink everything, I started to get considerably more done in considerably less time.

If it feels like the reason you're avoiding doing something is that you don't have the time, check the assumption for yourself. If it turns out to be true, then feel free to take it off your list – you're not avoiding it, you're just not prioritizing it.

But if it turns out to be a lovely story you tell yourself, consider dropping the story about why you're not doing it and get on it, get into it, and get it done!

———

What did you get off your list today?

WEEK TWO: TIPS, TRICKS, HACKS, AND HINTS

"One of the great challenges of our age, in which the tools of our productivity are also the tools of our leisure, is to figure out how to make more useful those moments of procrastination when we're idling in front of our computer screens."

– Joshua Foer

DAY EIGHT: WHAT A SUPER COOL PRODUCTIVITY TOOL!

Have you ever noticed how much we love the idea of a good productivity tool?

In fact, I suspect some of you may have jumped ahead to this week as it sounds like I'm going to tell you the magic bullet answer to all of your productivity problems (for the low, low price of only $9.99 for the basic package, $49.99 for the advanced version, or $99.99 for the super-deluxe package).

And if so, I apologize for the deception. But the problem with most time productivity tools and time management systems is that they take as much or more time to manage as it would take to just do the tasks they're designed to track.

That's not to say tools can't help – I'm a big fan of Google Calendar and Superhuman email and have played around with dozens of other paper and online systems over the years.

But ultimately, the only measure of a productivity tool is whether or not it makes you more productive. And for most of us, a pen and paper or the notes app on our phones is more than enough to handle the number one challenge in getting [sh]it done.

———

As productivity guru Dave Allen says:

> "The stress [of getting things done] is not from having too much to do; it's from not knowing what it is."

He goes on to say:

> "Your mind is for having ideas, not holding them."

———

So here's your super cool productivity tool for the day – no extra charge:

Get your to-do lists out of your head (in any way that appeals) so you can bring a relatively quiet and spacious mind to getting [sh]it done in the world.

———

What did you get off your list today?

DAY NINE: WHY DEADLINES (SOMETIMES) WORK

Nearly all time management systems are based on the idea that time is a fixed quantity and we all get access to roughly the same amount of it. There are sixty seconds in an hour, twenty-four hours in a day, seven days in a week, etc. But you can't put time in a wheelbarrow, which means that time is less subject to the laws of physics than it is to the principles of how the mind works.

Or to put it another way, time is a concept we've made up to help us coordinate action and make sense of things in the world. And deadlines work (when they work) because they temporarily alter the way we make up time.

Have you ever marveled at how much you're able to get done in the days or hours leading up to a vacation?

Here's what I've seen about how that works when we have a deadline approaching that we take to heart...

———

1. Life becomes more black and white

When we take a deadline to heart, we simplify our priorities down to the bare minimum. The answer to questions become "yes", "no", or "I can't think about that right now". Our standards are temporarily lower and getting [sh]it done becomes more important than how well it gets done. Good enough, at least for the moment, becomes a good enough standard for our work.

———

2. We're less inclined to indulge our thinking

It sometimes seems as though people (and sometimes life itself) wait until we're really, really busy to dump a ton of additional "to-dos" on our plate. But when a real deadline approaches, we seem to be able to put aside our complaints against the universe long enough to get what needs to get done done.

———

3. We let the small stuff take care of itself along the way

A popular analogy for priority management is the story of a professor who places a large jar on the table.

By the side of the jar he places a bucket of gravel, a bucket of sand, a bucket of water, and three big rocks. He then challenges his participants to find a way to fit everything on the table into the jar.

After numerous attempts, it became clear that the only way to fit everything in is to start with the big rocks first. The gravel fills the space between the big rocks, the sand fills the gaps in the gravel, and the water fills the gaps between the sand.

In the same way, when we put our attention on the big rocks in our life and don't let ourselves get caught up in the daily gravel, ground down by the sand, or swept away by the water, it's amazing how much of what we thought we had to do "just happens" while we're busy with what matters most.

So how do you put this to work in your pursuit of clearing out the backlog of things you've been avoiding doing?

My favorite way is to simply decide when I want to be done for the day and let that serve as my "deadline" for whatever things I've put on my list. Best case, I finish up each day on time and with a sense of satisfaction for a job well done; worst case, I finish up each day on time with at least one or two less things on my "Things I'm avoiding doing" list than I had when my day began.

———

What did you get off your list today?

DAY TEN: "DONE" LISTS

As part of our annual ***Creating the Impossible*** challenge, I often invite participants to begin keeping a "done" list – a list of everything they have actually done that day, regardless of whether or not it began its day on a list.

This is the opposite of a "to do" list – your list will get longer as the day goes on instead of shorter. But by the end of each day, you wind up with a pretty clear sense of how much (or how little) you've actually been prioritizing the things you've been avoiding doing and how much (or how little) time you've spent doing other things instead.

Instead of using the list to judge yourself, I recommend just noticing what you notice and carrying on with the exercise. In my experience, within a week of simply paying attention by writing it down, your priorities begin to change "all by themself" and more things start disappearing off your "Things I'm Avoiding Doing" list then ever before.

———

What did you get off your list today?

DAY ELEVEN: THE MILLION DOLLAR QUESTION

I n my early work with clients, I remember being surprised at how often someone would say they wanted to do something and then come up with incredibly plausible-sounding stories about why they couldn't. It was often not obvious to me whether or not the stories were actually true, but it was obvious that they believed them and would pass a lie detector test defending them.

So I came up with something I call "the Million Dollar question":

If I were going to offer you a million dollars for the successful completion of any task on your list, would you get it done? How would you do it? When?

About 95% of the time, people quickly saw through their stories and set about completing their tasks; the other 5% of the time they either realized they really were unable to complete it (which then allowed them to take it off their list), or they really didn't want to complete it, they just thought they should.

For today, check anything that's still on your list of things you're avoiding doing and ask yourself the Million Dollar question:

If I were going to offer you a million dollars for the successful completion of that item, would you get it done? How would you do it? When?

In most cases, you'll at the very least get past the idea that there's a real-world obstacle holding you back. And if it turns out that you really do want to make it happen, you probably will.

———

What did you get off your list today?

DAY TWELVE: THE SMITH & WESSON STRATEGY

As you may have guessed from the title, today's chapter is going to use some pretty dramatic (if unrealistic and completely fantastical) metaphors. If you're squeamish about violent mental imagery, you might want to give this one a miss. On the other hand, if you enjoyed Squid Games, the John Wick movies, or pretty much anything ever directed by John Woo, we should be good to go! ☺

While sometimes we just need a little bit of encouragement to get started on an action, for some of us having something to move away from can get us out of our heads and into action as well.

For example:

- If you knew that anyone who arrived late to a meeting would be killed, would you prioritize leaving home earlier and arriving on time?

- If you knew that the difference between your loved ones living and dying was your ability to complete everything on your "Things I'm Avoiding Doing" list by the end of the day, would you put your heart and soul into completing your list?

Unpleasant though these images might be, a lot of things that we think of as "impossible" suddenly become extremely possible if someone has a real or metaphorical gun to our heads.

So here's "the Smith & Wesson strategy":

What could you get off your list today if you put a metaphorical gun to your head?

Now I'll be honest – while such a mentally aggressive approach can certainly reap results in the short term, the main problem that I have with this as a daily strategy is that it quickly becomes unsustainable.

While the author Steven King reportedly used to motivate himself to write by imagining terrifying monsters screaming at him until he drowned out their voices with the sound of his typing, for most of us, if we keep putting a gun to our heads over time, one of two things happens:

1. We realize that it's an idle threat, and it stops "working" to get us into action.

2. We get so stressed by the whole thing that we kind of want to pull the metaphorical trigger.

So while you're welcome to give this a go today and see what comes off your list, I suggest you save it up as a strategy for (very) occasional use only... 😊

———

What did you get off your list today?

DAY THIRTEEN: MY FAVORITE TRICK TO GET [SH]IT DONE

I first learned this simple trick from my friend Steve Chandler, author of the wonderful book *Time Warrior*:

1.Get two pieces of paper. (I like to use the top two pages of a 'Post-it' pad, but it really doesn't matter!)

2. On the first page, write the words '"The only thing I have to do today is..."

3. On the second page, write out a fairly comprehensive version of your "Things I'm avoiding doing" list.

4. When it's time to begin working through your list, choose one item off the list to work on first. Rewrite it on the first page, making sure it's an action and not a "mini-goal". For example:

———

The only thing I have to do today is...

FINISH WRITING DAY THIRTEEN

———

5. Actually do whatever you have written down as if it's the only thing you have to do today.

6. When you complete that item, cross it off both lists.

7. Repeat steps 4 – 6 as needed!

———

What did you get off your list today?

DAY FOURTEEN: NOW IS HOW

One of my favorite books to read and re-read is a bit of wisdom fiction called *A Rich Man's Secret* by Ken Roberts. In the book, a man goes looking for the secret behind an old gravestone that is marked with the mysterious words:

66 *Take the first step, no more, no less, and the next will be revealed.*

As the story progresses, he learns about the wisdom of a wealthy businessman and philanthropist named Clement Watt, who ascribes his success and happiness in life to understanding that all we have is the present moment, but fortunately it's also all we need.

Whenever someone asks the businessman how he accomplished the many things he accomplished (including creating a unique breed of blue roses), his answer is consistent:

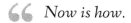 *Now is how.*

I've found the same thing to be true in my own life. Things that seem difficult and even impossible when I think about them inevitably succumb to my showing up in the moment, responding to what comes to mind, and seeing what happens.

So if there's anything left on your list either because you just don't know how to do it or how you'll ever get it done, try taking it out on a date. Spend some time with it. Get to know it. Bring your best self to it – the warm, funny, twinkly version of you that inevitably gets a second date because you had so much fun on the first one.

And see what happens. The projects you get done and things you complete might just be your own... 😊

———

What did you get off your list today?

WEEK THREE: A WHOLE NEW WAY OF THINKING ABOUT PROCRASTINATION

"I never put off until tomorrow what I can possibly do the day after.

-Oscar Wilde

DAY FIFTEEN: THERE'S NO SUCH THING AS PROCRASTINATION

Chances are that if you're reading this book, you're someone who considers yourself a bit of a procrastinator. But what I've seen over the years is that *there's no such thing as procrastination*. In other words, "procrastination" is not a mental or physical ailment - it's simply the label we hang on any situation in which we disapprove of the way we've chosen to prioritize our time.

For example, if I watch an episode of a new series on my favorite streaming service when I think I should have been working on my big project, I call it procrastination; if I don't think I should be working on my big project (or I don't have a big project to work on), I call it "watching a show".

The number one time management trick I've seen over the years to help people "overcome" this mythical thing called procrastination is to use some version of an A, B, C priority list.

Generally speaking, A's are "must dos" – those things that are both urgent and important. B's are usually "should dos", in the sense that they're either important but not urgent or urgent but not all that important. Finally, C's are "that'd be nice to dos" – they're neither important nor urgent but they do sound fun!

The problem with this kind of ABC prioritization is that most of us have developed the habit of trying to trick ourselves into getting things done by creating imaginary or self-inflicted consequences for not completing a not urgent and/or not important task. In other words, we take something we either want to do or think we should do and tell ourselves we have to do it.

Here's the test:

Are there any real-world consequences to not getting this done today?

If the answer is "yes" and it's a consequence you want to avoid, like losing your job, paying a fine, going to jail, etc, then by all means leave the task on your urgent list and get it done.

If the answer is "kind of", what that usually means is that the potential consequences of not completing the task are psychological and/or emotional – things like "I'll feel bad", or "it'll mean I'm lazy", or "it'll prove that I'm not motivated and disciplined enough to succeed".

And hey, nice try – pat yourself on the back for trying to motivate yourself through self-inflicted mental and emotional pain, but know that you will almost certainly continue to "procrastinate" on this task until it either becomes genuinely urgent or you genuinely want to do it and/or get it done.

While it might seem like being honest with yourself about what really needs to be done each day will lead to avoiding things even longer, it actually goes a long way towards feeling better about what you do accomplish over the course of a day.

In addition, when you allow yourself to spend as much time each day on what you actually want to do (as opposed to what you keep telling yourself you need to get done), you may well find yourself taking the right action at the right time in the right place with the right people.

––––––––

What did you get off your list today?

DAY SIXTEEN: WHY NOT JUST CONTINUE TO AVOID THINGS?

In my work with clients, I've found it helpful to distinguish between two kinds of things you're avoiding doing.

The first are those that either actively bother you, or that you can ignore for a little while but they niggle away at you in the background and take up valuable headspace. I call these things "bugs" - because they bug us - and like to mark them on my list with the Macauley Culkin/Edward Munch emoji 😱.

The second are the things you're just never going to get around to doing no matter how much other people think you should. While I don't really have a name for these and will probably never get around to coming up with one (see what I did there?), I can kind of encapsulate my feelings for them with a "shoulder shrug" emoji 🤷.

To help sort between the two for yourself, go through your list and see how many of your items you actually care about whether or not you get done and how many you don't. What may start out as a subtle feeling of difference between them will become more and more obvious as you go. Ultimately, you can just eliminate the "shoulder shrug" items from your list because you know you'll never get around to them so there's no need to keep then on a list.

As for your "bugs", the reward of getting them off your list is two fold:

1. First, they're usually still on your list because they're genuinely worth doing.

2. You'll be surprised at how much mental energy they've been taking up in the background that you get back when you get them off your list.

Here's a quick visual from Brendan Loper (@b_loper) I found on Instagram that illustrates the second point:

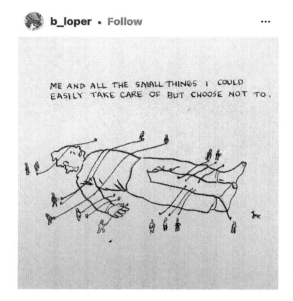

What did you get off your list today?

DAY SEVENTEEN: HOW TO MAKE SOMETHING A PRIORITY

O ne of the things I've learned over the years about getting [sh]it done is this:

The most important choice you ever make is what you choose to make important.

So the difference between what gets done and what doesn't is often more about intention and priorities than possibilities or circumstances.

If you want to prioritize something from your "Things I've been avoiding doing" list, here are three simple steps to get it done.

1. Do it first

One of the simplest ways I know to prioritize something is to begin with it – to put it right at the top of the agenda and stick with it until it's done. This approach seems to work particularly well with both actions and "mini-goals" – i.e. things that can be completed within the course of a few minutes to a few hours.

2. Do it now

I've yet to meet the person who isn't blown off course during the course of a day. In fact, no matter how many Post-It notes you stick on your computer, fridge, and dashboard, I guarantee you'll forget about your chosen priorities again and again. So the next time something from your list comes to mind, see if you can just do it now and get it off your list for good.

3. Do it often

How do you eat an elephant? One bite at a time. How do you prioritize something on your list that's going to take more than a few minutes? By coming back to it again and again and again (and if necessary, again.)

Play around with prioritizing things from your list today and notice what you notice – worst case, you just might find yourself getting stuff off your list and into the world!

———

What did you get off your list today?

DAY EIGHTEEN: 3 KEYS TO GETTING [SH]IT DONE

The best time management systems, as I've said before, are the ones that take the least time to manage. But what all of them have in common, at least to the extent that they help, can be summed up in just three words:

1. Clarity

In Alice in Wonderland, young Alice has the following exchange with the Cheshire Cat:

"Would you tell me, please, which way I ought to go from here?"

"That depends a good deal on where you want to get to," said the Cat.

"I don't much care where -" said Alice.

"Then it doesn't matter which way you go," said the Cat.

Whether you are using a goal-setting system, ABCD priorities, the 80/20 rule, or the Four Quadrants, the goal of most systems is simply to get you clear on what matters most in your world. And the clearer you are about where you want to go, the easier it will be to get there.

2. Structure

Have you ever wondered why you never get around to work on your novel or make progress on your "Wow!" goals but you pretty much always find time to brush your teeth and take out the trash?

As best I can tell, it's because we have a structure in place for teeth brushing and trash dumping that we're not continually experimenting with or trying to make better.

When it comes to getting stuff done, all helpful structures roughly break down into one of two categories – external reminders and personal routines.

An external reminder might be an appointment in your diary, an alarm set to go off when it's time to begin or end a task, or even getting an accountability buddy.

A personal routine is simply a habit that you get yourself into over time that becomes sufficiently ingrained that you don't have to think about it – it just doesn't feel right to finish your day without having done it.

3.Boldness

No matter how clear your priorities and how helpful your structures, how much of your getting stuff done list gets done is down to doing it, regardless of what circumstances the world happens to throw at you on any given day. While most people find it easier to boldly say 'yes' to their priorities and 'no' to the apparent demands of their boss, spouse, children when they have a socially acceptable deadline (like hard to get concert tickets or a plane to catch), you can say yes and no just as easily for no apparent or apparently justifiable reason.

Here's a simple rule of thumb:

The number of reasons you have for doing (or not doing) something is inversely proportional to how much you actually just want to get it done.

What did you get off your list today?

DAY NINETEEN: WHAT IF IT DIDN'T MATTER AS MUCH AS YOU THINK?

I n 30+ years of coaching humans (and 50+ years of being one), it's become obvious to me that one of the reasons people avoid doing things is because they're terrified about what seem to be the momentous consequences of their success or failure with the task at hand.

For example, when my son Oliver was about 12 years old, he began playing Pee Wee football. While he was actually one of the better players on the team in practice, he rarely played well in the games. After a few conversations, it became apparent that the problem was he was absolutely terrified of messing up, particularly as his coaches kept telling him that making even one mistake could cost his team the game.

My parental coaching "intervention" with Oliver was simply to show him one of my favorite video clips and encourage him to use the mantra shared in the video as his own. He did, and while it didn't turn him into an NFL superstar, it certainly helped him be as good in the games as he was in practice and even begin to enjoy himself in the process.

Here's a link to the clip — it's just over two minutes long and worth every second of your time...

https://bit.ly/meatballsclip

————

What did you get off your list today?

DAY TWENTY: INDISCRIMINATE ENJOYMENT, PART ONE

I was speaking with my friend and mentor George Pransky once about productivity – what it is that causes us to get more (or less) "bang for the buck" out of everything we do. One of the observations that came up was that people are generally at their most productive in the parts of their work where they like what they do and least productive in the parts of a job or project that they dislike, resent, or even hate. In fact, one study into people who had been at or near the top of their field for a minimum of twenty years showed that the one thing they all had in common was that they had figured out what they didn't like doing and stopped doing it.

But what if outsourcing the things. you've been avoiding doing isn't a viable choice?

If you can't afford (or don't want) to get someone else to do the bits of your work you don't like doing, you probably do what most people do – procrastinate for as long as you possibly can, and then when your really have to do it, you get it over with in the least painful and quickest way you can think of.

For example, Ben Cohen and Jerry Greenfield, the founders of Ben and Jerry's ice cream, reportedly hated firing people so much that the only way they could do it was by thinking of their business as a monster. Before getting rid of a slow-scooping employee, they would go in the back of their restaurant and chant "the monster is hungry; the monster must eat". Then they would begin to growl until they generated sufficient confidence to go out front and send their soon to be ex-employee packing.

While "getting it over with" is certainly more productive than never getting to something in the first place, it's certainly not an efficient long-term strategy. And things done with a white-knuckle "just gotta' get through it" frame of mind rarely go as well as they could. So what's the alternative?

Simple.

Begin to like everything you do.

Now at first glance, this seems to be a patently ridiculous idea. After all, how do I make myself enjoy catching up on a backlog of email, making cold calls, asking the bank for money, or whatever part of my work I think of as a "necessarily evil"? But what we like and dislike – i.e. our preferences – are not written in stone. In fact, most of them are the somewhat arbitrary result of childhood incidents, cultural conditioning, and psychological reinforcement.

As a girl, my wife was forced to drink warm milk that had been sitting in the sun in the school yard and it made her physically ill. That experience was passed on to our kids, who grew up hating milk without ever really having tried it. But in my house, we grew up enjoying milk in our breakfast cereal, milk with our after-school snacks, and a glass of milk with our dinner. And my sister's adult children still drink milk every day. The point, of course, isn't whether or not people should drink milk – it's that so much of what we like or don't like is based on limited or even second-hand experience, perpetuated unwittingly by the thought that "I don't like that".

I'll share a couple of real-life examples in part two, but for today, ponder this:

If you're avoiding something on your list because you

*think you won't like doing it, are you willing to let go of
your best guess and find out for yourself?*

———

What did you get off your list today?

DAY TWENTY-ONE: INDISCRIMINATE ENJOYMENT, PART TWO

Yesterday I shared a surprising secret behind getting [sh]it done – liking everything you do.

Here's a real-life example:

Francine came to me for coaching on growing her new business. She felt she needed to get better at networking in order to get clients, but as she told me in no uncertain terms, "I hate networking. It's fake, and it's phony, and it's just a bunch of people pretending to be interested in someone so they can make money from them."

When I gently pointed out that it wasn't surprising that someone who thought networking was evil wouldn't be terribly good at it, she upped the stakes by making her preference a character issue.

"I'm just not the kind of person who can lie, even when it would be in my own best interests. I've tried to fake being interested in people in the past, but it's just not me!"

While the amateur psychologist in me wanted to dive into the content of pretty much everything she said, the professional coach in me knew that the solution wasn't in the specifics of her thinking but in her misunderstanding of how Thought works. Thought is the paint with which our reality is created. We think and speak that paint onto the canvas of our consciousness, and then experience the painting as if it's real. But no matter how many times you've painted the same picture, it's still just one of a million possible pictures that could be painted on the blank canvas of the next moment. And no matter how "photo-realistic" your preferences look, they're still made up and painted by you. They're a representation of a possible reality – one tiny sliver of an infinite creative potential.

I told her the story of when the abstract painter Pablo Picasso was traveling on a train with a wealthy businessman who criticized his art as being "unrealistic". When Picasso asked him to explain, he took out a photograph of his wife from his wallet. "This is my wife, as she is", the businessman exclaimed. Picasso examined the photograph and then looked at the man wryly. "She's very small, your wife. And a bit flat."

My point was that we think we know what things are really like, but we only know what we think. And the wonderful thing about thought is that it can change in the blink of an eye.

Although Francine seemed a bit more settled when we had explored things for a bit, she was still uncomfortable with the idea that she was supposed to lie to herself and convince herself that she liked something that she didn't. "I'm just shy by nature," she explained.

"Are you?" I asked. "I've never met a shy baby. In fact, it seems to be completely natural for babies and small children to be indiscriminately fascinated by life. Which would at least suggest that enjoying everything is what's natural and having strong preferences is learned some-where along the way. What if you did your best to take all your thinking about networking off your eyeballs and came to it fresh?"

We spoke a few more times in the ensuing months, and she shared that to her surprise, she not only no longer hated networking, she found herself talking about her work with complete strangers on a regular basis and had picked up several new clients along the way.

And this is the wonderful possibility for all of us — the realization that we're not stuck with our acquired preferences and that we can return to our natural mode of indiscriminate enjoyment in any moment. Each time we get past our thinking and into whatever it is that we are doing, we learn more and do better. Over time, that indiscriminate enjoyment leads to less stress, less procrastination, and a natural boost in our productivity.

What did you get off your list today?

WEEK FOUR: FINISHING STRONG

"It's not so important who starts the game but who finishes it."

-John Wooden

DAY TWENTY-TWO: ARE YOU FINISHED YET?

I f you've been following the program day by day (and it's perfectly OK if you haven't), today I wanted to check in with you and see if you're actually finished with your list yet. While you may have had a litany of things or even just one or two larger-scale projects, it's entirely possible that your list is now empty or you've passed the point of no return – the tipping point where it would be harder to stop yourself from completing your list than it is to keep going.

If that's you, congratulations!

You're under no obligation to complete the program, because it was only ever designed as a catalyst to spark your own insights into and action towards the things you'd been avoiding doing. Hopefully you've at least begun to realize that most things succumb more quickly to action than psychology, and doing whatever it takes to get started on something is all it takes to get it done.

If not, not to worry – we've got another full week together of interesting and inspirational creative sparks to play with!

———

What did you get off your list today?

DAY TWENTY-THREE: THE FINISH LINE PHENOMENON

I n *Creating the Impossible,* I share some research into the psychology of happiness and success by positive psychologist Shawn Achor. In identifying the point at which the brain releases higher than normal amounts of endorphins and dopamine to help us complete a task, he noticed that it inevitably corresponded to the appearance of an apparent "finish line".

In other words, when the end is in sight, we get an internally generated chemical boost which provides the extra energy needed for a sprint to the finish. In my own work, I've come to see that this boost doesn't so much come from seeing an actual finish line, but rather from the hopeful thinking that real or imagined finish line engenders.

What also helps is that we inevitably simplify our priorities, losing ourselves in the energy of completion and saying an incredulous "no" to things that normally might distract us from the task at hand.

Here are a couple of questions that will help you incorporate the "finish line phenomenon" into the completion of your own list:

- What actions would you take today if you could actually see the finish line of your list or project on your list approaching?

- What would you focus on and what would you feel free to ignore if you knew that you could get it all done within the next 72 hours?

———

What did you get off your list today?

DAY TWENTY-FOUR: TIME IS NOT A VARIABLE

One of the most helpful things I've come to see about time and productivity management is that when it seems like we don't have enough time to get [sh]it done, we're missing the point.

Putting aside for the moment that there's no such thing as time in nature (and you can't put it in a wheelbarrow, which suggests it's made of thought), we all get the same 24 hours a day, 168 hours a week, 730ish hours in a month, and 8,760 hours in a year. (That's 525,600 minutes for fans of the musical Rent.)

So while how busy we feel is largely a function of our thinking, how full or spacious our calendar is 0% to do with time and 100% to do with what we try to squeeze into it.

I first started seeing this on my nightly dog walks, where I realized to my amusement and dismay that I was trying to sort out global warming, feeding hungry children, the third-quarter numbers for my business, and my kids love lives in a chunk of time that was just about perfect for my dogs to walk, pee, and poop.

When I abandoned my mental to-do list and got back to the present moment, I not only started enjoying the walk, I found a couple of ideas floating into my head that were actually actionable when the time came to actually action them.

How is this relevant to you and our shared quest to get the things we've been avoiding doing done?

Chances are that when you look at (and especially when you think about) your list, it feels a bit over-whelming. You start doing background "time math", calculating how long each thing on your list is going to take and contextualizing it in your mental calendar of other pressing appointments and activities.

But if you get clear that you never have to complete your list – just take the next action – you'll find the feeling of overwhelm mysteriously disappearing. And the more you just show up in the moment and do what there is to be done, the more of a sense of ease and flow you'll begin to experience not only with your list, but with your life in general.

———

What did you get off your list today?

DAY TWENTY-FIVE: USING OVERWHELM AS A PRODUCTIVITY TOOL

A lot of the mini-exercises and experiments I've offered up over the course of our time together are in the "little and often" category, where you effectively peck your list to completion – sort of the productivity management equivalent of "death by a thousand paper-cuts".

Assuming you've still got things left on your "things I'm avoiding doing" list, I'd like to invite you to try the opposite. Here's how I wrote about it in the form of a dialogue between a coach and a client in *Creating the Impossible*, adapted with permission from Steve Chandler's book *The Story of You*:

66 "Do you want to reach your impossible goal?"

Well, yeah, that's why we're working together. Do you know how I can do it?"

"Sure, I know how you can do it."

"Well, how?"

"Overwhelm it."

"What?"

"Overwhelm it."

"Well, what exactly do you mean by that?"

"Well, take massive action from a wild high-energy state that dwarfs the goal and overwhelms it. Be inappropriate to the goal."

"You want me to be inappropriate?"

"I do."

"In what way?"

"Don't take the appropriate amount of action. Take action that is absurdly disproportionate to the goal. Embarrass the goal. Knock it out of the universe. Smash it, slaughter it, and atomize it with crushing action. Go crazy on it. Beat it to a pulp. That's my advice."

Today, and throughout the week ahead, consider ignoring your loved ones, moving to a cabin (real or metaphorical) in the backwoods of Maine or Sweden (whichever is closer), and focusing in on your list until it's completely done.

(But of course if that doesn't appeal for some reason, you can always just do a little bit more than you normally would and see what happens... 😊

———

What did you get off your list today?

DAY TWENTY-SIX: IT CAN'T BE THAT SIMPLE

For a number of years, I have taught my students and trainees what I call "the simplest coaching model in the world":

1. Show up

2. Respond to what shows up

When they assure me that "it can't be that simple", I offer to go into a bit more detail.

When I say "show up", I mean that to be effective as a coach, you need to actually be in the same time and space as your client. That means you want to have as little on your mind as you can (so you're relatively undistracted). No hidden agendas, no roles you're trying to play, no one you're trying to impress.

In that real-time present-moment space, everyone does as well as they're going to do. They gain access to a real-time responsive intelligence that seems to know what to do and when and how to do it.

That in turn allows you to respond intuitively to what shows up both as an idea occurring in your own mind and in the words and actions of the other person.

While this usually begins to make sense to people, it can take a while before they trust that showing up and responding to what shows up is not only surprisingly effective, it's possible in any situation for any human being at any time.

So here's how this applies to you:

What if all you ever need to do is to show up to the next item on your list and respond to what shows up in your mind and world?

While you might think that it can't possibly be that simple... what if it is?

———

What did you get off your list today?

DAY TWENTY-SEVEN: BEING DONE

My wife and I love to watch a cooking competition called The Great British Bake Off. There's always a great bit when they do the final countdown: "Ten, nine, eight..." and everyone is rushing to put the last little bits on their cake and then "...three, two, one, step away! And they have to step away from their cake, or all their work up to that point will have been in vain.

And that's the final part of any endeavor. You step away from the cake (or project or list) either because someone has told you to or you've decided to and you... are...done!

How do you know when you're done with something you've been avoiding doing?

When you let it go.

In some formal systems of project management they talk about this phase as "meeting your conditions of satisfaction" and "declaring completion" It's a pre-determined point at which a documented list of every expectation required to meet success in a project has been met and signed off on by every stakeholder.

But that's always seemed unduly complicated to me when a simpler rule of thumb is this:

You're done when you say that you're done.

Today, go through anything left on your list and decide which items you're willing to let go and be done with for now. Being done with something isn't the same as avoiding it. It's simply the decision to take something off your plate, at least for now, so you can get on with what's new and fresh.

By way of example, I spent years thinking that I needed to finish every book I started reading and watch every movie I started until the end. But then one day it dawned on me that there are more books and movies already in existence than I will ever be able to watch, not even taking into account the fact that new ones are coming into the world every single day. So to stub-bornly make myself finish everything I started was less of a positive character trait than a kind of self-imposed torture device.

Please understand, you don't have to take anything off your list until you're ready. But make no mistake – you get to decide when you're ready – no one else. And most people I know feel a delicious sense of relief when they finally let themselves off the hook for something they have no intention of getting done in the first place...

———

What did you get off your list today?

DAY TWENTY-EIGHT: INSIGHTS AND IMPACT

One of the things I always enjoy doing when a project or experiment comes to a close is to take some time to review what worked for me, what didn't, and what I learned insightfully along the way.

You can do this review in your head, or you can just use a notebook, journal, scrap of paper, or note-taking app on your favorite device.

Here are some questions I like to ask to jumpstart the review process:

- What have you actually done over the past four weeks? What got created? What got eliminated? What got done?

- How does the whole category of "things I've been avoiding doing" look differently to you now?

- What was your favorite thing that happened along the way?

- What have you learned about getting [sh]it done?

- What have you learned about yourself?

I want to congratulate you on making it to the end of the program and I hope you had fun, learned heaps, and got a ton of [sh]it done. But before you go, I've got a few final thoughts for you...

AFTERWORD

HOW TO HAVE MORE FREE TIME (NO MATTER HOW BUSY YOU THINK YOU ARE)

"In order to accomplish anything truly worthwhile, it is necessary to be slightly underemployed."
-James B. Watson

———

Years ago I had a client whose relative lack of success was a mystery to me. He was smart, good with people, and had all the relevant education and qualifications in his chosen field of study to set himself up for a long career. But somehow no matter how many times we spoke, he made about as much progress as a runner on a treadmill, clocking up the hours without actually getting anywhere.

What finally resolved the mystery and allowed him to move forward was a simple time analysis, where I asked him to track his activities in 15 minute intervals over the course of the week. To my shock, he was spending as many as 10 hours a day "thinking about my biggest problem".

What was even more surprising, however, was that when I pointed this out to him he shook his head sadly.

"I know," he said, a bit guiltily. "I should be putting in another 2 – 3 hours a day thinking about it if I ever really want to solve it, but I just don't have the time."

I pointed out to him that spending hours trying to think your way out of problems is like walking east looking for a sunset - no matter how smart you are and how hard you're willing to work, it's never going to happen that way.

To explain this further, I shared my own story with him.

When I was 41 years old, I had an epiphany while listening to a video lecture by an enlightened Scottish welder named Syd Banks. Syd said that "Every human being is sitting in the middle of mental health – they just don't know it." For some reason my mind went completely quiet and I saw the simple truth of that. Like everyone else, I was born happy, and it was obvious to me that despite at least 30 years battling depression and 7 years struggling with suicidal ideation, there was nothing fundamentally wrong with me.

To say that seeing that threw me is a massive understatement. I didn't know what to do with myself, not least because I was about to undertake a book tour promoting my latest writings on how even if you were "naturally" depressed or anxious there were things you could do to have a pretty great life anyways.

I found myself with epic amounts of free time in what I had thought was going to be one of the busiest periods of my life, and I had no idea how to fill them. In the end, I spent more time with my wife and kids, read everything I could about Syd Banks and "the Three Principles of Mind, Consciousness, and Thought" that he wrote about, and beat every level of Angry Birds with three stars.

While I mostly enjoyed the slower pace of life this epiphany gifted me, I was also puzzled. Bear in mind, I was still embarked on a six-month book tour with a full coaching practice and weekly teaching commitments around the world. So where was all this free time coming from?

In order to make sense of that, let's try an analogy:

Imagine you were raised in an ancient culture which believed that in order for the sun to successfully rise and set each day, it was necessary for you, the strongest, fastest person in the village to go out to the farthest reaches of the countryside on horseback at dawn, awaiting the sunrise. As soon as the first light appeared in the East, you threw invisible lariats as far and high as you could, each lariat made by hand by the medicine man of your village from a golden light too fine for the human eye to see. Once you caught the sun in their snare, you took off on horseback and began pulling the sun through the sky,

This activity would continue until midday, at which point you would need to cut the golden lariats free and instead hoist a 30 foot tall scare crow and ride on behind the sun, now chasing it the rest of the way across the sky until it left your people in peace for the night.

Each day the sun successfully rose and set would be a victory for both you and your people, and while the work might be exhausting and at times backbreaking, your sense of accomplishment each time you basked in the sun over the fields at midday and chased it out of the sky at night let you sleep restfully, despite any worries you might have about having to do it again the next day lest the sun never again rose to its dizzying heights or never left the sky, forcing either endless days or endless nights.

Then one day, a wise shaman from a neighboring village arrived and announced that there was a deeper intelligence at work in the universe, and that the sun would surely rise and set without any effort on your part. Most people laughed at the shaman and a few suggested burning her at the stake, but somehow you, in your heart of hearts, recognized the truth in what she was saying.

The next morning, despite the voice in your head screaming at you to get out of your bed and go to work, you lay awake instead in your bedroll and waited to see what would happen. To your surprise, delight, and horror, the sun completed its journey through the sky without any help or interference from you.

Surprise, because instead of your inner recognition of the truth of the shaman's words, there was still a part of you that needed to see it with your own eyes to truly believe it. Delight, because to bask in the glorious light of the sun without any responsibilities for its success or failure is a truly delightful way to spend one's time. Horror, because it occurs to you how much time you've wasted trying to make something happen that was always already happening whether you knew it or not.

While the village elders simply replaced you with another rider and gave thanks to the gods that despite your taking a day off, their village was blessed with a full day of sunlight nonetheless, you sought out the shaman to give thanks.

When you find her, you look into her eyes and find yourself without words, as though the very sun you spent your life pulling through the sky resides within her as well. She looks at you knowingly and shares these words of wisdom:

"Like the sun, the light of life is always within you. There is nothing you can do to hasten its rise and nothing you can do to chase it away."

You look deeply into her face and finally see that the light in her eyes is merely a reflection of the light emanating from your own. You embrace and return to your life, calmer, wiser, and with more free time than you know what to do with...

As we come to the end of this book together, I'd like to thank you for your willingness to spend some of your valuable life-time with me. I hope it has proven both helpful and enlivening.

As the things you've been avoiding doing get done (or simply taken off your list because you no longer feel the need to convince yourself you need to do them), you'll find yourself with more mental bandwidth and more free time.

If I have earned the right to offer you one last piece of advice, here it is:

Don't fill up your free time and take up increased bandwidth with a whole new set of projects and to-do's. Let yourself be slightly underemployed. Do less, better.

With all my love,

Michael

ACKNOWLEDGMENTS

Writing may be a solitary activity, but creating a book takes a village. Lynne Robertson is the leader of the Caffeine for the Soul Press village, and without her vision, creativity, and relentless work ethic the world would be a poorer place.

This book would also not exist without the inspiration of my son Oliver, for whom the original program was created, nor without the hundreds of participants in that very first group, who offered real-time feedback on which things made the biggest difference in clearing the backlog in their lives.

I have been fortunate in my life to be mentored by a number of truly inspiring and insightful people - particular thanks for their sparking my thinking in the realm of productivity goes to Steve Chandler, Mavis Karn, and George Pransky.

Last (but by no means least), I would like to acknowledge my wife Nina for being my constant companion, confidante, and friend over the past thirty plus years of exploration. We've come a long way, baby, and hopefully have an equally long adventure ahead of us!

ABOUT THE AUTHOR

Michael Neill is an internationally renowned transformative teacher, author, broadcaster, and speaker.

He has spent more than three decades as a coach, adviser, friend, mentor, and creative spark plug to founders, CEOs, celebrities, royalty, and those who are up to something in the world.

A gifted communicator, Michael has authored six best-selling books including *Creating the Impossible*, *The Inside-Out Revolution*, *The Space Within*, and *Super-coach*. His books have been translated into 26 languages, and his public talks, retreats and seminars have touched and transformed lives at the United Nations and in over 60 countries and on six continents.

His TEDx talks, 'Why Aren't We Awesomer?'and 'Can a TEDx Talk Really Change the World?' have been viewed by over two million people and his blog and podcast, Caffeine for the Soul, has been entertaining and inspiring audiences around the world for more than 20 years.

ALSO BY MICHAEL NEILL

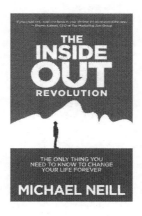

The Inside-Out Revolution: The Only Thing You Need to Know to Change Your Life Forever

Would you like to experience amazing clarity, peace and freedom, even in the midst of challenging circumstances?

In this ground-breaking new book, bestselling author Michael Neill shares an extraordinary new understanding of how life works that turns traditional psychology on its head. This revolutionary approach is built around three simple principles that explain where our feelings come from and how our experience of life can transform for the better in a matter of moments.

The Space Within: Finding Your Way Back Home

There is a space within you where you are already perfect, whole, and complete. It is pure consciousness - the space inside of which all thoughts come and go.

Every problem we have in life is the result of losing our bearings and getting caught up in the content of our own thinking; the solution to every one of those problems is to find our way back home. This is both the invitation and the promise of this book.

One problem. One solution. Infinite possibilities. Are you ready to begin?

————

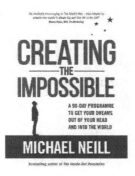

Creating the Impossible: A 90-day Program to Get Your Dreams Out of Your Head and into the World

Thousands of people from all over the world have already used his 90-day programme to reconnect with their creative spark and get their most important ideas and projects out of their head and into the world. Now it's your turn...

What if you could accomplish more than you ever imagined without the constant stress and pressure associated with 'high achievement'?

What if creating what you want to see in the world isn't dependent on believing in yourself, or even believing that it's possible?

Whether you want breakthrough results for your business, yourself or your life, this book will change the way you see yourself as you learn to make the impossible possible!

Supercoach: 10 Secrets To Transform Anyone's Life

Join best-selling author and internationally renowned transformative coach Michael Neill as he guides you through 10 coaching sessions designed to change your life for the better.

Inside you'll learn:

· a simple but profound explanation of how the mind works

· why happiness is closer than you think

· a whole new way of thinking about goals

· the simple foundation of lasting relationships

· a radical new understanding of human emotion

· the secret to financial security in any economy

· ideas to spark your creativity, productivity, and so much more!

A User's Manual
For Human Beings
By Mavis Karn
With a Foreword by Michael Neill

It's That Simple: A User's Manual for Human Beings

by Mavis Karn

"One of the wisest people I know..."

-Richard Carlson, #1 NYT Bestselling Author of the *Don't Sweat the Small Stuff* series

WHEN'S THE LAST TIME YOU FELT THE WAY YOU WISH YOU COULD FEEL ALL THE TIME?

In this wonderfully simple yet profound book, professional counselor and teacher Mavis Karn, author of the letter to kids (and former kids) known around the world as "The Secret", shares lessons learned from over 45 years of working with individuals, families, schools, businesses, hospitals, prisons, professional athletes, and teams.

If you've ever wondered why you can be on top of the world one minute and ready to give up the next, how it is that some of your best ideas come when you least expect them, or how to find true peace of mind in the midst of a chaotic world, this "user's manual for human beings" will leave you saying "it can't be that simple!"

But what if it could?

Mavis Karn is a counselor/educator/consultant in private practice in St Paul, Minnesota. She is also a mother, grandmother, and great-grandmother.

A Rich Man's Secret: A surprisingly simple secret for success by Ken Roberts

Take the first step - no more, no less - and the next will be revealed...

With these words, carved into the headstone of a mysterious gravestone, one man's search for the secret to a life well-lived takes him on an adventure into the spiritual truths hidden in the midst of our ordinary lives. If you enjoyed books like *The Alchemist*, *The Celestine Prophecy*, and *The Way of the Peaceful Warrior*, this timeless classic will gently guide you back to yourself and show you how simple it can be to make your way profitably in the world.

"This book changed my life!"

-Michael Neill, international bestselling author of *The Inside-Out Revolution* and *The Space Within*

Combining homespun wisdom with deep spiritual truth, *A*

Rich Man's Secret is a heartfelt look at the quiet trials and tribulations we all experience in our pursuit of happiness and success. Ultimately, it is the story of an ordinary human being who stumbles across the surprisingly simple secret to leading a truly rich and worthwhile life.

FREE BONUS VIDEO - FALLING IN LOVE WITH GETTING [SH]IT DONE

You made it!

As a thank you for making it all the way to the end (or a reward for cleverly skipping the book with all it's time-consuming content and jumping ahead to this bit :-), I'd like to gift you with a free video called **Falling in Love with Getting** [Sh]**it Done**.

Here's all you need to do:

1. Go to www.michaelneill.org/tiad-book and order the program

2. Enter the code **TIAD24** at checkout

3. Enjoy your video session!

Printed in Great Britain
by Amazon

53340640R00073